W9-ABY-468

START EXPLORING™

The American West

A Fact-Filled Coloring Book

EMMANUEL M. KRAMER

ILLUSTRATED BY HELEN I. DRIGGS

RUNNING PRESS
PHILADELPHIA · LONDON

NO LONGER THE PROPERTY
OF THE
UNIVERSITY OF R. I. LIBRARY

Copyright © 1995 by Running Press.

Printed in Canada. All rights reserved under the Pan-American and
International Copyright Conventions.

*This book may not be reproduced in whole or in part in any form or by any means, electronic or
mechanical, including photocopying, recording, or by any information storage and retrieval system now
known or hereafter invented, without written permission from the publisher.*

Canadian representatives: General Publishing Co., Ltd.,
30 Lesmill Road, Don Mills, Ontario M3B 2T6.

9 8 7 6 5 4 3 2 1
Digit on the right indicates the number of this printing.

ISBN 1–56138–585–9

Cover, interior, and poster illustrations by Helen I. Driggs
Cover design by Toby Schmidt
Interior design by Susan E. Van Horn
Edited by Brian Perrin
Poster copyright © 1995 by Running Press.

This book may be ordered by mail from the publisher.
Please add $2.50 for postage and handling.
But try your bookstore first!

Running Press Book Publishers
125 South Twenty-second Street
Philadelphia, Pennsylvania 19103–4399

CONTENTS

PART 5

The "Indian Wars"

PAGE 58

PART 6

Law and Lawlessness in the Wild West

PAGE 74

PART 7

Great Figures and Legends of the West

PAGE 90

PART 8

National Parks and Monuments of the West

PAGE 110

PART 1

The Land and the Coming of the People

Millions of years ago, a vast sea covered the western regions of the United States. Over the centuries, as the sea wore away the surrounding mountains, great quantities of sand and minerals settled on the sea bed. There, the enormous weight of the water compressed them into sandstone and limestone.

Pressures within the earth later thrust up these layers of stone, pushing back the ancient sea. As the waters retreated, a new landscape was exposed. Then, many thousands of years ago, during the last Ice Age, great rivers of ice called *glaciers* (GLAY-sherz) rolled over this landscape. The glaciers were like giant bulldozers, carving deep valleys and leveling large tracts of land as they moved. This is how the great plains of the American West were formed.

The Ice Age ended about 12,000 years ago, but the forces of nature—especially wind and water—continued to shape the western landscape into the form we see today.

Rivers formed as the ice receded and dug deep valleys in the earth. One of the most famous features of the West, the mile-deep Grand Canyon, was carved by the Colorado River as it wound its 1,400-mile course from the snowfields of Wyoming and Colorado to the Gulf of California in Mexico.

Other rivers carved paths of their own, creating a sculptured landscape of spectacular stone formations. Today, the United States government preserves some of these sites of incredible natural beauty in our National Parks and Monuments.

Thousands of tourists now visit these places every year, but who were the first visitors to the American West? For centuries after the European discovery and exploration of the New World, this was a great mystery. Nobody knew just how or when people first came to the Americas. One popular theory was that Native Americans descended from the inhabitants of the lost continent of Atlantis!

Then, at the beginning of the twentieth century, an African-American cowboy made an important discovery that would change the way scientists thought about the origins of the first Americans.

Erosion formed Arizona's mile-deep Grand Canyon over hundreds of years as the Colorado River wound its long course from Wyoming to the Gulf of Mexico.

THE FIRST AMERICANS: FOLSOM CULTURE

One dusty day in 1908, a lone cowboy rode his horse through a narrow canyon near Folsom, New Mexico. Suddenly, something sticking out of the canyon wall caught his eye. Dismounting for a closer look, George McJunkin discovered some very mysterious bones. They looked like animal bones, but were larger than any he had ever seen.

The bones belonged to a species of prehistoric bison that had become extinct more than 10,000 years ago. Archaeologists digging at the site uncovered more bones from animals that vanished near the end of the last Ice Age. McJunkin's bones were a major find, and helped establish when human beings had first come to the Americas. The presence of so many bones in one place suggested that a group of people had hunted, killed, and butchered these animals, but the archaeologists wanted better evidence. Then, in 1927, after further digging, they found a stone spearhead embedded in the rib bones of a kind of bison that had been extinct for nearly 12,000 years. This proved that people, too, lived in the Americas at least that long ago, and that they had hunted large game near Folsom.

Later, bones found close to spear points in other areas confirmed that groups of early hunters had lived throughout the Southwestern United States. Scientists reasoned that these people must have migrated to America from Asia, following herds of migrating animals across a land bridge that existed during the Ice Age between what are today known as Siberia and Alaska.

These prehistoric hunters were *nomads* (NOH-madz)—people who never settled in one place. They roamed the land, following animals to places where kills could be made. Evidence of their culture has been found from Alaska to Tierra Del Fuego, on the southernmost tip of South America.

More than 12,000 years ago in the American West, prehistoric people hunted animals such as the 8-foot-tall, moose-like *Sivatherium*.

THE CANYON DWELLERS

Deserted stone structures, mysterious ghosts of past societies, sit in the walls of canyons throughout the Southwest. No one is sure what became of the tribes that inhabited these structures.

The canyon dwellers were descendants of the nomadic tribes that first migrated to the Americas from Asia. Over time, the nomads learned how to cultivate the land so that they no longer had to move with animal herds to have food. Growing crops such as corn, beans, and squash, they began to settle in villages. In addition to the foods they grew, the villagers gathered fruits, nuts, and berries, and hunted smaller game, such as deer, rabbit, and turkey.

By 500 A.D., these people began to settle in the natural caves found along the stone walls of canyons. They dug circular pits in the earthen floors of the caves, and covered them with mud-plastered wooden frames to build structures known as pit houses. A pit house was entered through an opening in the roof, which also served to release smoke from the fire.

Later, around the year 700 A.D., the canyon dwellers began to move out of the pit houses. They built large communal dwellings on the flat tops of *mesas* (MAY-suhz), the long ridges of land at the top of canyon cliffs. In some areas of the Southwest, they constructed stone communal houses—buildings that sheltered many families—in canyon valleys.

For reasons still unclear to archaeologists, this plan of communal living was eventually abandoned, and people returned to the shelter of the caves. At this time, they began to construct stone dwellings, towers, and *kivas* (KEE-vuhz). Kivas were underground circular structures similar to pit houses. Their secretive chambers were used for worshipping the spirit world and weaving ceremonial clothing.

By 1300, many of the cliff dwellings had been abandoned. The tribes that inhabited them—the *Anasazi* (AH-nuh-SAH-zee) and *Mogollon* (MOH-guh-YOHN) —probably moved on to other lands, but it is a great mystery what became of them. The stone-and-mud architecture of their canyon civilizations has endured and is an impressive sight today.

Early Native Americans of the Southwest built underground *kivas*—mysterious circular structures in which they worshipped the spirit world and wove ceremonial clothing.

PART 2

Spanish Culture in the Southwest

In 1540, Spanish explorer Francisco Vazquez de Coronado set out from Mexico on an expedition through the Southwest. Moving through lands that are now the states of Arizona and New Mexico, Coronado encountered a number of Native American villages. He named these villages *pueblos* (PWAY-blowz), the Spanish word for towns.

THE PUEBLOS

The inhabitants of the pueblos were also called *Pueblos*. They built their houses out of *adobe* (uh-DOH-bee), or sun-dried mud bricks, and arranged them in clusters several stories high. Wooden ladders on the outside of the buildings allowed people to climb to the higher floors. In case of enemy attack, the Pueblo people could take refuge in the upper stories of their homes and pull the ladders up behind them, making it difficult for the attackers to reach them.

The Pueblos probably descended from the cliff-dwellers who once inhabited the canyons of the Southwest, and many aspects of their lives resembled those of their ancestors. The Pueblos built kivas for sacred ceremonies in their earthen homes. For food, they raised corn, beans, and squash in the fields around their towns.

The Pueblos used a wide, flat milling stone called a *metate* (meh-TAH-tay), and a hand-held grinding stone called a *mano* (MAH-no), to grind corn into flower for bread, which they baked in small clay ovens. They were also skilled potters. Brightly colored pots with intricate designs were used in every household for storing grain or water.

The Pueblos resisted Coronado's attempts to conquer them. Led by seasoned warriors, they fought courageously, and the Spanish soon learned they were formidable adversaries. Eventually, the Pueblos talked Coronado into leaving by telling him incredible tales of the "Seven Cities of Gold"—fabled cities that could be found elsewhere in the Southwest. The Spaniards moved on in search of the imaginary wealth of these cities, but would later return to conquer the pueblos.

The Pueblo people, such as these Navajo farmers, built their homes of adobe
and raised crops in the fields around their towns.

THE GREAT PUEBLO REVOLT

In 1598, another Spanish explorer, Juan de Oñate, conquered New Mexico in the name of Spain. As Spanish soldiers moved into the area, life changed drastically for the Native Americans of the Southwest.

Missionaries followed in the wake of the soldiers and converted many Pueblos from their ancient religion to Christianity. Spanish soldiers received land grants that included the Native Americans living on the land. Although orders came from Spain that the Pueblos were to be treated kindly, most of the Spanish governors ignored the message.

The Pueblos quickly became slaves who labored in the fields and mines, or built mansions and churches for their new masters. The Spanish overseers forced the Pueblos to work more than sixteen hours each day, with little or no time to rest. They frequently beat the workers with whips, and if they felt they were not working hard enough, they took away their food and water as punishment.

By 1680, the Pueblos had had enough abuse and oppression. They met secretly to organize a revolt against the Spanish rulers. In the bloody uprising that followed, the Pueblos burned the mission churches and killed the priests who had forced them to give up their religious traditions. Many Spanish colonists fled their estates, but those who remained were killed and their lands and animals were taken by the Pueblos.

The rebels even succeeded in taking over the governor's palace in Santa Fe. The Spanish authorities were overwhelmed and retreated with the landowners to El Paso, in present-day Texas, where they began to prepare a counter-attack.

The Great Pueblo Revolt lasted for thirteen years. During that time, the Pueblos regained their dignity and their land. But the Spanish were armed with superior weapons, and they eventually began to win back the Pueblo lands. Many Native Americans were killed by the attacking soldiers; others died from starvation and thirst as the Spanish trapped them in their villages and cut off their water supplies. By 1693, the Spanish once again controlled New Mexico.

In the seventeenth century, Spanish conquerors made slaves of the Pueblo people,
and forced them to work long hours with little rest.

THE SPANISH LEGACY

The Great Pueblo Revolt took place in New Mexico, but the reconquest of the pueblos served to strengthen Spanish rule in a much wider area, including what are now the states of Arizona, Utah, Colorado, Nevada, and California.

The centuries of Spanish rule in these areas left their mark on the art and architecture of the Southwest. Towns established under Spanish authority were all organized according to similar plans. They were built around a main square or plaza, with the governor's mansion on one side and the main church on the other. A marketplace and soldiers' barracks were built on the other two sides.

Most of the buildings were made of adobe, which was cheap and readily available. The mud brick walls were often plastered over to prevent rain water from turning the bricks back into soft mud. The roof was built over long logs called *vigas* (VEE-guhz), which extended over the edge of the walls. Smaller strips of wood, called *latias* (LAY-shyuhz), were set over the vigas to cover the roof. Finally, tree branches were packed over the latias, and the entire roof was sealed with adobe mud.

Churches, too, were built with adobe. To give special value to the mud bricks used in churches, the priests ground up precious stones and poured expensive wines into the mud mixture. The early churches were simple box-like structures, with two bell towers in front. Later churches added elaborately carved stonework around the entrance.

The interior of a Spanish church was filled with the paintings and carvings of Spanish folk artists. A large screen carved of wood and painted with various religious scenes stood by the altar. Carved wooden statues of religious figures, called *Santos* (SAN-tohss), lined the aisles.

To preserve their Spanish colonial heritage, many southwestern cities today require that buildings in the town center remain in the adobe style. Mission churches that once stood in ruin have been restored, and the art works from their interiors are preserved in museums.

This adobe cathedral in Santa Fe, New Mexico, is typical of the
Southwest's Spanish-style architecture.

THE BATTLE OF THE ALAMO

One hundred and eighty-two Americans lay dead, slaughtered by Mexican forces under the command of General Santa Anna. The site of this great tragedy was a mission church in San Antonio, Texas, called the Alamo.

In 1821, Mexico won independence from Spain and took control of the southwest territories that were once part of the Spanish empire. These territories included Texas. The Mexican government invited people from the United States to settle in Texas, hoping U.S. settlements would help stop raids by Native Americans. Settlers were promised large grants of land and plenty of space to raise their families.

President Andrew Jackson wanted to buy Texas and make it part of the United States, but his offer of $5 million was rejected. The American settlers grew to resent Mexican authority. They did not understand the Mexicans and felt superior to them. This attitude was a source of great tensions between Americans and Mexicans.

As more settlers from the U.S. poured into Texas, things got worse, and the Mexican authorities sent in soldiers to control the area. Among the American settlers, a movement to become independent from Mexico began to form. Minor skirmishes between American settlers and Mexican troops followed. In an attempt to strengthen the American presence, the settlers placed advertisements in U.S. newspapers asking for volunteers to come to Texas with rifles in hand. Two such volunteers who came to aid the settlers were frontiersmen Davy Crockett and Jim Bowie.

Preparing for war, a force of American settlers under the leadership of Colonel William Travis took up a position in the Alamo, thinking the church would make a good fort. In March of 1836, a force of nearly two thousand Mexican soldiers attacked the Alamo. The fort's defenders fought courageously, but they were overrun, and no one survived.

The legendary bravery of those who defended the Alamo made them heroes to Americans everywhere. American forces, rallying to the battle cry of "Remember the Alamo," went on to defeat the Mexicans. In 1847, the Southwest became a part of the United States.

The defeat of American settlers at the Alamo took the United States
into a full-scale war with Mexico over Texas.

PART 3

The United States and the Exploration of the West

At the beginning of the nineteenth century, the great western wilderness was largely unexplored. Long before becoming president in 1801, Thomas Jefferson decided it was important to gain control of the western territories. He feared the British might occupy regions west of the Mississippi River and use them as a base for fighting the young United States.

THE LOUISIANA PURCHASE

During Jefferson's presidency, France was waging costly wars in Europe and needed money to fund its conquests. To raise the money, French General Napoleon Bonaparte offered to sell the port of New Orleans to the United States. President Jefferson immediately sent delegates to France to conclude the deal.

Imagine the delegates' surprise when Napoleon offered to sell them the entire Louisiana Territory! This was an enormous territory that stretched from the Mississippi River to the Rocky Mountains, and from Canada to Mexico. It was an offer that could not be refused, and the Louisiana Purchase of 1803—a bargain at $15 million—doubled the size of the United States.

Even before the Louisiana Purchase, President Jefferson had planned an expedition to find the *Northwest Passage*. This was a water route from the Mississippi River to the Pacific Ocean that people hoped existed. If it did exist, it would save months of travel time for ships sailing from the Atlantic Ocean to the Pacific. Jefferson appointed his private secretary, Meriwether Lewis, to organize and lead the expedition. Lewis's mission was to find the Northwest Passage and explore the vast, unknown Louisiana Territory. He chose his friend William Clark to help him lead the expedition. The epic adventures of Lewis and Clark became one of the most exciting chapters in the history of the American West.

President Jefferson appointing his private secretary, Meriwether Lewis, to organize an expedition to explore and chart the Louisiana Territory.

THE LEWIS AND CLARK EXPEDITION

Drawing their bows, the party of Teton Sioux (TEE-tawn SOO) warriors declared that the group of about thirty men would not be allowed to continue up the Missouri River. Angered by this attempt to put a halt to their expedition, Meriwether Lewis and William Clark stood firm. Clark drew his sword, and the Sioux warriors, seeing the guns of the twenty-six soldiers standing behind him, backed down. It was a close call, and fortunately, no one was hurt.

Lewis and Clark had been sailing up the Missouri River for five months when they met the Teton Sioux at the mouth of the Bad River in present-day South Dakota. They had set out May 14, 1804, from St. Louis, their boats weighted down with gifts for the Native Americans they expected to encounter. The river, with its shallow sand banks and hidden logs floating beneath the surface, was difficult to navigate.

One of the most important missions of the expedition was to establish good relations for the United States with Native American nations. Lewis and Clark wanted to tell Native Americans about the Louisiana Purchase and persuade them to send representatives to meet with U.S. officials in St. Louis. Aside from the encounter with the Teton Sioux, Lewis and Clark were very successful. Several tribes sent their chiefs down the river on official visits.

The expedition spent the winter among the Mandan (MAN-dan) tribe in what is today Bismarck, North Dakota. Here, Lewis and Clark met the young Native American woman Sacajawea (sa-ka-ja-WEE-ya) and her French-Canadian husband Toussaint Charbonneau. Sacajawea and her husband joined the expedition as guides and interpreters.

Continuing their journey in the spring, the expedition reached the Great Falls in Montana in June 1805. It took the explorers two weeks to carry their boats and equipment around the falls. They built rough carriages, using slices of logs for wheels. They placed the canoes on these and pulled them over the land by rope.

But the most grueling part of the journey was yet to come—the trek across one of the continent's greatest natural barriers, the Rocky Mountains. As they prepared for

Lewis and Clark confronting the Teton Sioux at the mouth of the Bad River, in what is today the state of South Dakota.

the crossing, Lewis and Clark encountered a Shoshoni hunting party. Sacajawea, who had been captured from the Shoshoni (show-SHOW-nee) tribe when she was a child, discovered that the party's leader was her brother!

The Shoshoni tried to discourage the expedition from attempting to cross the mountains. But when they saw that Lewis and Clark were determined to push on, they helped them by supplying them with the pack-horses they needed for the crossing.

Braving hazardous weather, dangerous climbs along steep cliff walls, and food shortages that threatened them with starvation, Lewis and Clark and their team crossed through the Rockies in September. Then they sailed up the Clearwater and Snake Rivers, facing rapids and rocks that threatened to destroy their boats.

In spite of incredible obstacles, the travelers sailed down the Columbia River to the Pacific coast in November 1805. They headed back east in the spring of the following year, carrying with them vast amounts of useful information in the form of maps and journals kept by Lewis and Clark and members of their party.

They also carried back important samples and descriptions of plant and animal life that had never before been available for eastern scientists to study. Easterners had heard of the grizzly bear, for example, but Lewis and Clark were the first to describe it in detail and give it a scientific name: *Ursis horribilis*.

During their great journey, Lewis and Clark charted a region that had been a mysterious and vast wilderness to most Easterners. The tales of their travels made them into living legends, and the information they provided opened up the American West to further explorations and settlement over the next century.

Lewis and Clark and the members of their expedition carrying their canoes
and supplies across the Rocky Mountains.

LONE WILDERNESS EXPLORERS: THE MOUNTAIN MEN

In the thirty years following the ground-breaking Lewis and Clark expedition, lone animal trappers seeking furs to sell back in the East explored the western mountain ranges extensively. The trappers, often called "mountain men," were a strange breed. They roamed the wilderness with two horses, one for riding and the other to carry their supplies. They dressed in animal skins and grew long beards. Their skin, because of its long exposure to the sun and wind, looked like worn leather. Many trappers lived among Native American tribes and married Native American women.

A serious problem for these hardy souls was the danger of being attacked by bears. So mountain men carried large knives, rifles, and molds for making their own bullets. In spite of these arms, stories of trappers being mauled and killed by bears were common.

The pelts of beavers were very valuable back in the East. The fur of this large rodent was used as a trimming for many styles of women's dresses, as well as for making felt for hats. Mountain men carrying sacks full of iron traps would venture into wilderness areas and set their traps in beaver ponds. They often trapped in the early spring, after the beavers' fur had thickened over the winter months. Beavers caught in the traps usually drowned, though some would actually chew off their trapped legs to escape.

Then, each summer, the trappers would bring the furs they had collected to special locations. There, fur company representatives paid them their very handsome and hard-earned rewards.

Each time they returned to civilization, the mountain men brought more information about what was to be found in the great western wilderness.

In the 1800s, rugged mountain men wandered the western wilderness, collecting animal furs to sell back east.

John Colter

John Colter was a soldier who made the long voyage with Lewis and Clark from St. Louis to the Pacific Coast. He stayed with the expedition for part of the return journey, but headed west again in 1806, serving as a guide to two fur trappers.

Colter stayed in the western wilderness for the next four years, often working as a hired guide and trapper for Manuel Lisa, an adventurer from St. Louis. In 1807, he guided Lisa and a group of other trappers to the point where the Yellowstone and Bighorn Rivers meet in Montana. Here they built a fort, and Colter left the group to set out on explorations of his own. In search of new trapping grounds, he roamed the mostly unexplored lands that now make up the states of Montana, Idaho, and Wyoming.

During his wanderings, Colter was captured by a band of Native Americans from the Blackfoot tribe. As a kind of sport, the Blackfeet forced him to run for his life while he was chased by warriors armed with spears. Running barefoot over rocks and thorns, Colter managed to kill one of the warriors. Then he escaped by jumping into a cold river and swimming to freedom.

Colter returned from his lone explorations with incredible stories of the spectacular geysers, boiling mud pots, and hot springs he had seen in the northwest corner of present-day Wyoming. But Colter was one of the first white men to witness these natural wonders, and almost nobody believed him. Skeptical Easterners dismissed his stories as a mountain man's tall tales, and began calling the region "Colter's Hell."

His discoveries roused great interest in the region, however, and later expeditions confirmed the sights he described. Almost immediately, a movement to preserve this fragile natural wonderland was undertaken. The result was the creation of Yellowstone as America's first National Park in 1872.

After surviving another attack by the Blackfeet in 1810, Colter gave up his life as a mountain man and sailed 2,000 miles down the Missouri River to St. Louis. There he married and lived out the rest of his life as a farmer.

Wilderness guide and trapper John Colter set out to explore the Yellowstone region,
but encountered Blackfoot warriors and narrowly escaped.

Jim Bridger

Jim Bridger was only nineteen years old in 1823. That was the year he joined a party of trappers heading into the wilderness of the Rocky Mountains.

Two years later, already a seasoned mountain man, Bridger took a canoe down the dangerously rough waters of the Bear River that runs through Wyoming, Idaho, and Utah, to settle a bet about where it flowed. At the end of the river, he found himself on the edge of Utah's Great Salt Lake. Although he believed at first that it was the Pacific Ocean, Bridger was probably the first white man to see the lake.

Bridger was also one of the early visitors to "Colter's Hell" in the Yellowstone region. Like Colter, his descriptions of geysers, petrified trees, and boiling mud pots were all accurate, but not believed by people back east. His stories, too, were dismissed as the visions and fantasies of a mountain man who had spent too much time away from civilization.

Bridger spent much of his early days in the West as a trapper exploring every possible site for beaver pelts. Later, when too many trappers roamed the wilderness, and the beaver population began to die out, he became an army scout and an expedition guide and supplier.

Bridger never went to school, but he was skilled at mapping the regions he explored, and he spoke fluent Spanish and French. He also spoke several Native American languages, and his deep respect for Native American ways of life allowed him to develop good relations with the tribes he met. He married three times, each time taking his bride from a different tribe.

In 1843, Bridger set up a fort and trading post at a pass in the Rocky Mountains. Fort Bridger became an important stop on what was known as the Oregon Trail—one of several routes followed by wagon trains of pioneers migrating west. Here, pioneers could get their wagons repaired and restock their supplies for the final stretch of their long journey.

Trouble with arthritis and failing eyesight forced Bridger to retire in 1867, ending a career that stands out among the legendary adventures of the many mountain men who roamed the American West.

Explorer Jim Bridger navigating the Bear River that flows into Utah's Great Salt Lake.

JOHN WESLEY POWELL

Early maps of the West listed a section of Colorado River country as "unexplored territory." Major John Wesley Powell, a Civil War veteran who had lost an arm in battle, decided in 1869 to undertake an exploration of this area—one of the last uncharted regions of the American West.

Four boats had been transported west by railroad for Powell's expedition. Ten men were to accompany him on his exploration of the Colorado. Only six of those men would complete the dangerous river journey through the area we now call the Grand Canyon of Arizona.

It took twenty-six days for Powell and his party to pass through the Grand Canyon. The dangerous waters tossed about the men and supplies. Rocks in the rapids threatened to tear the boats apart. Only two of the four boats completed the trip. Battered by rapids and whirlpools, Powell's men were exhausted and hungry. Their clothing was torn to shreds in the struggle against the waters.

When they finally reached calm water, the men marveled at the awesome scenery that surrounded them. Spectacular stone formations stood all around them in the mile-deep gorge. Unusual types of plant growth decorated the canyon slopes. Animal life was everywhere.

All of this was of great interest to Major Powell, who was a professor of geology. The natural wonders of the Grand Canyon led him to gather scientific information about the region's resources. This information would help people find the best use for the land, as well as the best way to conserve its natural beauty.

Powell emerged from his adventure a national hero. He had conquered the mighty Colorado River and gathered a wealth of information. His findings led to the creation of several governmental agencies charged with managing the natural resources in the United States.

Today, the Glen Canyon Dam holds back the waters of the Colorado River. The waters behind the dam form an immense lake that flows into hundreds of canyon inlets, creating tall islands of stone that can be reached only by boat. The name of this great lake—Lake Powell—celebrates a man of great courage and accomplishment.

Major Powell and his expedition navigating the dangerous waters of the
Colorado River through Arizona's Grand Canyon.

PART 4

Westward Ho!

Mountain men like John Colter and Jim Bridger were some of the first Easterners to seek their fortunes in the West. But as fur trappers and scouts blazed new trails and made new discoveries, more and more Easterners moved west in search of better lives. Aside from animal furs, the riches of the West included fertile farmlands, gold, timber, and wide pastures for cattle. But long before Easterners came in search of these treasures, Native American populations living on the great plains of the West had treasures of their own.

BUFFALO

Buffalo played a very important role in the lives of Native American cultures in the Great Plains. The Great Plains are the flat, open lands that stretch from the Mississippi River to the Rocky Mountains, and from Canada down to southern Texas.

Every part of the buffalo had its use. The meat was cooked, dried, and mixed with berries to make a kind of jerky called *pemmican* (PEM-ih-ken). The Native Americans made weapons, tools, and pipes from buffalo bones. They used the buffalo hides to make teepees, clothing, moccasins, drums, and even boats. The tongues, livers, hearts, and skulls of the animals were used in religious ceremonies. The intestines were dried to make a kind of cord; buffalo hair was used for rope. Jewelry, glue, and utensils were made from the hooves. Cups, ladles, and spoons were made from the horns. Even buffalo dung was used for fuel!

Sadly, as more and more settlers moved west, they too discovered the value of the buffalo. Settlers made buffalo hides into warm coats and other leather products. Railroad workers killed buffalo for food. But the settlers were not as careful as Native Americans about how they used the buffalo. They killed more than they needed and let many parts go to waste. Huge numbers of buffalo were slaughtered by white hunters until the millions of buffalo that once roamed the region were reduced to merely a few thousand.

Sixty million buffalo once roamed the Great Plains, but today there are fewer
than 10,000 of these animals living in the wild.

THE OREGON TRAIL

One of the first treasures that drew people to the West was the land itself. Lured by tales of the rich, fertile valleys of the "Oregon Country" (Wyoming, Montana, Idaho, Oregon, and parts of California), thousands of eastern farmers and their families loaded their belongings into covered wagons and moved west in the 1840s.

The long and difficult route they followed—the Oregon Trail—had been forged by fur trappers roaming the Rocky Mountain country during the 1820s and 1830s. Wagon trains would set out from Independence, Missouri, swing northward to the Platte River, follow its course westward to cross the North Platte, then trek across a barren country to the Rocky Mountains. Moving southwest through a gap in the Rockies known as "South Pass," the wagons would emerge at Fort Bridger and follow the Snake River north to the Columbia River, which could be followed all the way to the Pacific coast.

The pioneers' ox-drawn wagons were not very sturdy. They were nothing more than wooden boxes covered with oil-cloth canopies and set over a frame on iron-rimmed wheels. Wagons were often washed away while crossing rivers, and settlers frequently drowned. The wheels would get stuck in muddy ruts, and the axles broke easily on the rough and jagged mountain passes. Trees and rocks had to be cleared from the path to prevent damage. Finally, the settlers had to reach their destination before the harsh winter months. Added to these dangers was the constant possibility of attacks from Native Americans, who were angered by the settlers' intrusion on their lands.

Disease, bad water, and exposure to cold weather caused countless deaths among the people of the wagon trains. More than 30,000 settlers were eventually buried in shallow graves along the Oregon Trail. To hide the graves from wolves and Native Americans, who might unearth them to collect trophies, no crosses or headstones were left. The pioneers would then run their wagons over the burial sites to erase all traces of recent digging.

In spite of all the hazards of the Oregon Trail, nearly 12,000 settlers had successfully made the nightmarish journey by 1848, when Congress created the Oregon Territory.

By the time Congress created the Oregon Territory in 1848, nearly 12,000 settlers had made the long and hazardous journey west on the Oregon Trail.

THE DONNER PARTY

In 1846, the families of prosperous farmers George and Jacob Donner, furniture manufacturer James Reed, and others, came together in Independence, Missouri, and set out for California on the wagon trails. Their journey would become one of the greatest tragedies of the overland crossings.

The travelers were full of enthusiasm for their long migration and the new lives they would find in California. A new book by Lansford W. Hastings, an unscrupulous land promoter, painted a rosy picture of the journey and of the wondrous lands that awaited on the Pacific coast.

The Donner party set out on the Oregon Trail with unrealistic expectations for an easy crossing. They traveled in large, luxurious wagons that were heavy with extra comforts.

The first part of the journey went well, but the huge group split up when it reached Fort Bridger on the western side of the Rocky Mountains. Here, the Donners and their party of 87 chose to take the "Hastings Cutoff." This was a short cut that Hastings described in his book. He claimed it would cut 400 miles out of the trip, but the route had never been tried with ox-drawn wagons, and it turned out to be much more difficult than Hastings suggested.

Before long, the Donner party found itself crossing a great salt desert. The harsh landscape took its toll on both people and wagons. Heat and thirst killed many of the cattle brought along for food. Some of the wagons were damaged beyond repair, and whole families had to walk and live without shelter.

The strain and hardship of crossing the desert left the pioneers weak, confused, and angry. Fights and arguments sprung up readily. James Reed was banished from the Donner party after he killed a man in a fight. His family secretly supplied him with food and a gun to help him survive alone in the wilderness.

By the time the Donner party reached the Sierra Mountains in California, the winter snows had begun, and they were trapped until spring. With inadequate

Members of the Donner party set out on the Oregon Trail in luxurious
wagons laden with extra comforts.

shelters and little food, they were now faced with starvation and fierce cold. As the winter wore on, the families ate the bark from trees and leather from their boots to stay alive.

In the meantime, James Reed managed to reach California. He organized a rescue mission and returned to save his family. But it was too late for the Donners and many others. Only forty-seven members of the group survived the horrible winter at what is now known as Donner Pass.

James Reed's rescue group found his wife and children among the few survivors. One of Reed's daughters, twelve-year-old Virginia, described her experiences in a letter to her cousin. "Never take no cut-offs and hurry along as fast as you can," she wrote as advice.

When the Donner Party's wagons became damaged crossing the desert, whole families were forced to walk and live without shelter.

GOLD FEVER

They were mostly young men who set out to seek their fortunes in the West, dreaming of discovering great wealth and living a life of ease. News of gold finds in California, Nevada, and Colorado lured thousands of Easterners to the gold fields where they would find great hardships and suffering. A lucky few reaped a harvest of gold.

Heavy mining required machinery that only major companies could afford. Individual prospectors had few tools for the difficult task of extracting gold from the rocky hillsides. Many of the young miners soon realized that they would not find the gold they were seeking. Some gave up and returned home with shattered dreams.

One of the most famous gold rushes began when a carpenter found traces of gold on the central California property of businessman John Augustus Sutter in 1848. When news of the discovery leaked out, Sutter's lands, not far from San Francisco, were overrun by gold seekers from everywhere. These prospectors were the first wave of what would become an enormous migration. The California Gold Rush of 1849 increased the population of that territory from 20,000 to 100,000 in just one year!

With rumors of new gold discoveries in the West, mining towns sprung up almost everywhere miners had staked a claim. Most of the towns featured bars where miners could find whiskey after a hard day of labor. Businessmen set up grocery stores and shops to sell supplies to the miners. Mining towns grew and expanded so quickly that they came to be known as *boom towns*.

Gold also attracted criminals to the West. Lawlessness became a part of life in the mining towns, and killings were common. The streets could be dangerous for law-abiding citizens.

Over time, most of the towns that grew up around mining claims died away. Today, the American West contains many such deserted towns where the wind and dust blow over abandoned buildings. These ghost towns are evidence of the shattered dreams of those caught up in the gold rushes of the late 1840s.

During the California Gold Rush of 1849, thousands of prospectors moved west in a quest for gold.

COWBOYS ON THE CHISHOLM TRAIL

Another treasure of the West lay in its wide open grasslands, where cattle ranchers could raise herds and make their fortunes selling cows to meat markets.

Large herds of cattle had lived in Texas for many years, but no one thought of selling them for meat until the 1860s, when new railroad lines made it possible to ship cattle to eastern markets. The next two decades saw the rise of dozens of prosperous *cow towns* in Texas and other parts of the great plains.

To get their cattle to market, cattlemen—sometimes called *cattle barons*—hired cowboys to herd them across the prairies to railroad centers in the midwest. These long journeys were known as *cattle drives*.

Nearly 1,500 miles long, the Chisholm Trail was the herding path that led from Texas to the railroad shipping centers of Kansas. As many as 3,000 cattle would make the long trip at one time, moving at an average speed of twelve miles a day.

Grazing along the way, the great herds moved along under the guidance of the cowboys. Usually, a *trail boss* directed the operation. The trail boss was aided by at least one cowboy for every three hundred head of cattle. Each cattle drive also had a cook, who fed the cowboys from his *chuckwagon*—a sort of kitchen on wheels.

The cowboys' work was difficult and exhausting. The men spent long hours in the saddle, keeping the cattle moving. Some of the herd animals developed sores on their feet or became ill, slowing down the cattle drive. Stormy weather, especially thunderstorms, could frighten the herd and cause a dangerous stampede. Despite these difficult conditions, the riders had to keep all of the animals moving together.

There were other hazards along the Chisholm Trail. Native Americans would raid the herds to steal some of the cattle and horses for their people. Some animals would be washed away by strong water currents when they swam across rivers. Buffalo herds would sometimes become entangled with the large cattle herds, and cowboys spent long hours separating the animals. Parties of cattle rustlers seized any opportunity they could find to steal some of the cattle.

Cowboys herding their cattle along the 1,500-mile Chisholm Trail in the 1870s.

To meet the challenges of the cattle drive, cowboys had to have many skills. They could rope cattle with their lassos and protect their herds from wolves and rustlers.

Back on the ranch, the cowboy had other duties. He had to inspect the land to be sure the cattle were not overgrazing the area. He had to treat cattle that were sick with worms, bitten by rattlesnakes, or stuck with porcupine quills. Before the invention of barbed wire fencing, he had to make sure the cattle stayed on the rancher's grazing land and that other ranchers' cattle stayed away.

Branding was another job that demanded a cowboy's great skill and quick timing. Bringing down a large cow would require two men and the tricky job of throwing a lasso in just the right way to snag the animal. Branding cattle was also a dangerous job—the kick of a cow could send the red-hot branding iron into a cowboy's face!

Most cowboys had as many as twelve horses helping them do their job. During a cattle round-up, one cowboy might use as many as three different horses in a day. Caring for the horses was another time-consuming job.

Cowboys worked long hours under hard conditions, leading lives that were much less glamorous than movies have led us to believe. It was a way of life that required resourcefulness and the patience to endure hardships without complaint. The hard work and endurance of the cowboys have made them heroes to generations of children and adults all over the world.

Cowboys had to keep the cattle together and on the trail as they herded them to railroad centers in Kansas. Here, a cowboy tries to lasso a runaway calf.

THE GREAT WESTERN FORESTS AND THE TIMBER INDUSTRY

It was something to write home about, and many did. Almost everyone who came to the West marveled at the great forests that stood between the Rocky Mountains and the shores of the Pacific Ocean.

There was a great need for timber. Wood was used to build houses for the increasing numbers of pioneers moving west. Mining companies needed timber to hold up the walls of their mine shafts. Railroad companies used wood to build the train tracks that were beginning to move into the West. Lumber also was sent overseas and traded in foreign ports to be used for building ships. Trees in the Northwest grew close to the ocean and could be cut and loaded directly onto boats for transport to all parts of the world.

The California Gold Rush of 1849 encouraged the timber industry to cut down huge tracts of forests. Gold miners were willing to pay whatever was asked for the lumber they needed, and they soon became the major buyers.

When trees were cut, loggers sent them to the saw mill by sliding them on long tracks known as *skid roads*. These roads were made up of small logs laid side by side and greased with fat. They were built running downhill so that the huge trees that were cut down would slide easily on their way to the mill.

When timber companies moved out of certain regions, poor people came to settle the area. Their settlements became known as *skid rows* because they grew up around the skid roads built by the lumber industry. Today, the term *skid row* means any very poor or run-down part of a town.

The loggers, or *lumberjacks*, who cut down the trees lived in timber camps in poor conditions. The bunkhouses where they slept were crowded, and the cookhouses where they ate were often dirty and unsanitary. Lumberjacks developed a reputation for being tough.

One of the biggest problems caused by the timber industry was *clear cutting*. This process removed all the trees at a given site and destroyed the homes of birds and animals living there. Back in the nineteenth century, few people were concerned by this, but today many environmental groups fight to stop clear cutting in our nation's woodlands.

During the 1800s, lumberjacks cut down trees in the great forests of the Northwest.

THE PONY EXPRESS

The large numbers of people emigrating to the American West in the 1800s needed a way to communicate with friends and family in the East.

In the 1850s, railroads and telegraph lines crisscrossed the East, making communication and long-distance travel relatively easy there. But delivering mail to the newly settled territories west of the Rockies was still a problem. There were no telegraph wires across the mountains, and rail lines linking the Atlantic and Pacific coasts were still years away.

One of the solutions to this problem was the short-lived but very famous Pony Express, which began service in 1860. Investors set up a route that would carry letters from St. Joseph, Missouri, to Sacramento, California, in just ten days. The nearly 2,000-mile course was divided into 190 stations where riders could change horses and pass mail on to fresh horsemen.

The idea of a service that would speed the delivery of mail across the West was doomed almost from the start, and the Pony Express was plagued by problems. Riders had to endure the hardships of bouncing along in the saddle for great distances. Ponies became strained and exhausted from the fast pace of the journey. Native Americans attacked the Pony Express stations, stealing ponies and often killing workers. Riders arriving at stations devastated by such raids had to continue on, straining themselves and their horses even more. Bad weather conditions slowed the pace of travel and delayed the delivery of mail. As a result, angry subscribers cut their payments, creating financial difficulties for the already troubled service.

Newly strung telegraph lines finally made long distance communication available to everyone. The first transcontinental telegraph came into service in 1861, and the death of the Pony Express soon followed.

Although it existed a short time only, the ambitious Pony Express experiment became a legendary part of the American West.

Pony Express riders sped the delivery of mail along the 2,000-mile
course from Missouri to California.

THE COMING OF THE RAILROADS

They came together one day in 1869 at Promontory Point, Utah, to drive a golden spike into a railroad cross tie. It was a great event that signaled the completion of the transcontinental railroad. After years of hard work, Americans finally had rail service connecting cities on the Atlantic Coast to the growing cities, cow towns, and boom towns of the West.

The building of the transcontinental railroad was a dramatic chapter in the history of the West. Workers for the Union Pacific Railroad company began laying track westward from Omaha, Nebraska, in 1863. Meanwhile, workers from the Central Pacific Railroad laid track eastward from Sacramento, California.

The Central Pacific crews had great obstacles to overcome. Crossing the Sierra Nevada Mountains meant dealing with snowstorms and dangerous mountain passes. They blasted tunnels through the rock at many points along the route.

The company had difficulty finding workers for this grueling job until it brought in 10,000 Chinese immigrants. Living conditions for the Chinese crews were unsanitary, and the pay was low. But they worked at a fast pace to complete their section of the rail line.

At the same time, working westward for Union Pacific were more than 10,000 other workers—many of them Irish refugees from a great famine that struck Ireland in 1848. A fierce competition developed between the Irish and Chinese crews, and made them work even faster until they reached their goal that day at Promontory Point.

The era of railroad building played an important part in America's expansion into western lands. By 1885, several transcontinental lines had been built. The federal government supported the railroads by giving them generous grants of land. States gave charters to rail companies, and even sold bonds to pay for the building of the railroads.

Trains carried essential goods, from clothing to pots and pans, for sale in the western territories. Soldiers and military equipment could be transported to areas where they were needed to fend off attacks by Native Americans. Perhaps most importantly,

The first transcontinental railroad was completed in 1869, when workers drove a golden spike into a cross tie connecting the Union Pacific and Central Pacific railroads.

the coming of the transcontinental railroad lines made it possible for settlers and visitors to travel to towns that had been difficult to reach before.

Trains made travel to the West easier and faster but not necessarily more comfortable, especially for those who could not afford to ride in first-class cars. Miners traveling to new claims, farmers going to town for supplies, and hunters heading off to new hunting grounds all used the railroads regularly. The cars they rode in had few conveniences. Passengers were often in danger of freezing in the cheaper, unheated coaches.

Traveling in luxury cars was more expensive. Inventor George Pullman built special railroad cars with soft seats and beds to serve the wealthy. "Pullman cars," as they became known, had sleeper beds, fancy curtains, and attractive wood furnishings. Elegant meals were also served to passengers on these trains.

Travelers in the early days of train travel faced many hazards. Flash flooding caused tracks to wash away and snowstorms trapped railroad cars in massive snow drifts. Fierce winds carried dust that soiled the travelers' clothes and caked onto their skin, irritating their eyes, noses, and throats. There was also the danger of Native American attacks and train robberies by western outlaws. Toward the end of the nineteenth century, travelers experienced a new menace: professional gamblers who rode the rails cheating people out of great sums of money.

In spite of all its hardships, train travel to the American West was a great improvement in the movement of people and supplies. Thousands of people headed west by train to build the towns and cities of the new frontier.

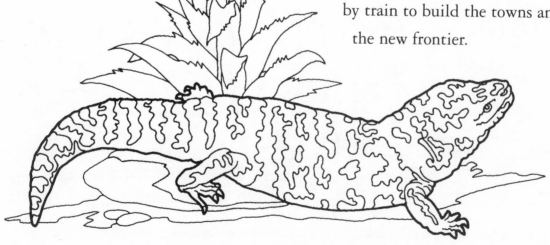

Trains made travel to the West faster and easier, and delivered supplies much more efficiently to the fledgling towns and cities of the frontier.

THE OKLAHOMA LAND RUN

At noon on April 22, 1889, a bugle call sent thousands of frenzied settlers racing across the plains of the "Indian Territory," now known as Oklahoma. Not even the feverish California Gold Rush of 1849 matched this incredible migration, which brought more than 60,000 settlers into the Indian Territory in a single day.

The Indian Territory had been set aside as a great reserve of land for Native American populations. The U.S. government forced the "Five Civilized Tribes"—the Cherokee, Creek, Seminole, Chickasaw, and Choctaw—to migrate there from other parts of the country. When the relocation ended, part of the territory—about two million acres—remained unused. This area became known as the "Unassigned Lands."

The Unassigned Lands were perfect for farming, and white settlers had long wanted to move in, but until the government decided to open the territory to them in 1889, whites were kept out by soldiers who patrolled the borders.

On the day of the great land run, the settlers came on horses, in wagons, on bicycles, on foot, and by train to stake their claims to the farmlands and town lots that were available. Because there were not enough plots of land for all of the settlers—known as *sooners*—they came with rifles, prepared to defend their claims.

The U.S. government opened up other tracts of land to settlement in the early 1890s, including six million acres called the "Cherokee Strip," on present-day

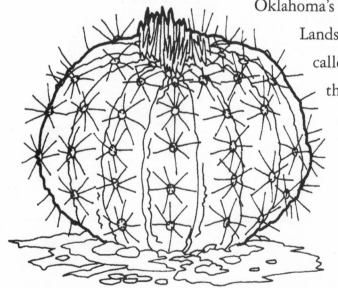

Oklahoma's northern border. As the Unassigned Lands were settled, they were reorganized and called the "Oklahoma Territory." In 1907, the Oklahoma and Indian Territories, with a combined population of about one and a half million, joined to become Oklahoma, the forty-sixth state admitted to the U.S.

In 1889, more than 60,000 settlers, known as *sooners*, came to Oklahoma April 22 to stake out claims to fertile farming lands.

PART 5

The "Indian Wars"

Native Americans living in the wide open spaces of the West believed that the land belonged to all people. They roamed freely and had access to all of nature's resources.

Easterners who migrated west refused to be bound by Native American beliefs about the earth and how people should use it. White settlers were eager to divide the western lands into separate plots owned by individuals. As they staked their claims and fenced in their land, conflicts between them and Native Americans became more and more common.

On the great plains of the West, Native Americans watched the white man kill the buffalo, their main source of food. White missionaries came to their villages and tried to make them give up their native religion.

The United States government entered into treaties that promised Native Americans they would not be driven from their sacred sites or traditional hunting grounds. But most of these promises eventually were broken. For example, when gold was discovered in the Black Hills of South Dakota, gold miners rushed in and staked their claims on lands that were protected by treaty.

As their way of life was threatened more and more, Native Americans fought back with raids against white settlers and attacks on wagon trains. The United States government ordered its military forces to solve the "Indian problem" by putting Native Americans on government-controlled reservations. Tribes were forced to give up their homes, camps, and sacred grounds, and move to these reservations.

This policy led to a series of wars in the West—known as the "Indian Wars"—that were eventually won by the United States government. But the West was not the only place where Native Americans were asked to give up their land and their lifestyle in favor of citizens of the United States. In the East, there had been problems, too.

Easterners moving to the West often crossed or settled Native American lands. This led to a series of conflicts and battles known as the "Indian Wars."

THE TRAIL OF TEARS

United States soldiers, armed with bayonets, stood in the doorways of the Cherokee's homes. Their orders were to relocate the Cherokee to new lands in the West.

The Cherokee had been living in Georgia as an independent nation—with their own schools, homes, and system of government—for decades. They were one of several Native American nations—the others were the Creek, Seminole, Chickasaw, and Choctaw—known as the "Five Civilized Tribes" who lived in the area and governed themselves.

Beginning around 1830, the U.S. government passed laws requiring these tribes to leave their homelands and move to the "Indian Territory" in what would later be known as Oklahoma.

Some of the tribes left their homes in the early 1830s, but the Cherokee resisted. Their Chief, John Ross, fought the U.S. government policy in court and took his case all the way to the Supreme Court. Unfortunately, he lost, and the soldiers came to evict his tribe in the late 1830s.

The Cherokee were forced to march all the way to their new lands on foot. Extreme cold, starvation, unsanitary conditions, and disease plagued the march. Camps established by the U.S. along the way did not provide enough food, blankets, or adequate shelter to help the Cherokee recover from their long, hard hours of walking. Almost one quarter of the Cherokee died on this sad journey, which has since been known as the "Trail of Tears."

Those who survived the long march settled in the new territories and tried to rebuild their civilization. They established a written alphabet to preserve their language in a tribal newspaper and through the new schools they set up. The schools also taught tribal traditions, dances, and games. But these efforts at preserving their culture were almost wiped out fifty years later when white settlers flooded the area during the Oklahoma Land Run.

After being forced from their homes by the United States Government, Cherokee from Georgia made the long march to their new lands as a U.S. Cavalry officer looked on.

FORTRESS ROCK

In 1861, Christopher "Kit" Carson—already a legendary adventurer who had explored much of the West—was put in command of a volunteer army. The group's mission was to round up the Native American tribes—Navajos, Apaches, Kiowas, and Comanches—who continued to fight white settlers in the Southwest.

After three years of successful campaigns, Carson sought to capture the last of the Navajo living in northern Arizona's Canyon de Chelly (de SHAY). Many of the Navajo (NAH-va-hoe) surrendered without a fight, but about three hundred refused. They took refuge on a 700-foot-high flat-topped rock known ever since as Fortress Rock.

The top of Fortress Rock was very difficult to reach. To climb to the top, the Navajo built wooden bridges over deep gaps in the rocky path and cut ladders and footholds into the rock. They carefully carried supplies of food and wood for fuel to the top and placed them in storage. To prepare for the harsh winter weather that was fast approaching, they built mud-plastered stone buildings.

Kit Carson set up camp on the floor of the canyon just below the high cliffs of Fortress Rock. There, he and his soldiers waited for the Navajo to surrender or starve to death.

Meanwhile, the Navajo survived comfortably, guarding the passes that led to the top of the rock, until a sudden drought caused a severe water shortage. They devised a plan to get water from a creek located on the canyon floor: in the dark of night, they formed a human chain that snaked down the steep rocky cliffs. They quietly collected water and passed the containers hand to hand back up to their cliff-top refuge.

But life on Fortress Rock became more and more difficult as the shortages of food and water grew worse. Finally, after more than four months, the Navajo were forced to surrender. In March of 1864, they joined thousands of other Native Americans in what became known as "The Long Walk." This was a 400-mile walk from Canyon de Chelly to Fort Sumner in New Mexico. More than 8,000 Navajo were forced to undertake the perilous journey, and many died of disease and starvation along the way. The Long Walk became another of the great tragedies of the wars between the United States and Native American nations.

Navajo who refused to leave their homes in Arizona's Canyon de Chelly camped out on Fortress Rock and passed badly needed supplies of water back up to their cliff-top refuge.

CUSTER'S LAST STAND

U.S. troops and Native American forces from many tribes fought dozens of battles in the 1870s and 1880s. The most legendary of these battles took place June 25, 1876, near the Little Bighorn River in Montana Territory.

On that day, Lieutenant-Colonel George Armstrong Custer, a Civil War hero known throughout the country, led 600 U.S. troops into battle against about 3,000 Sioux and Northern Cheyenne warriors. It was probably the largest force of Native American warriors ever assembled.

After marching his Seventh Cavalry unit forty miles, Custer approached a Sioux-Cheyenne village on the Little Bighorn. His scouts warned him of the size of the Native American force, but Custer ignored them. He also ignored orders from military command to circle and surround the village. Instead, he commanded his troops to divide into three separate groups that would attack the village from three different positions. This greatly reduced the strength of his force and set the stage for the slaughter that was to follow.

Custer and his forces were trapped and slaughtered by an overwhelming number of warriors. Not one of Custer's men was left alive. Known ever since as "Custer's Last Stand," the battle that took place that day—the Battle of Little Bighorn—was one of the greatest disasters in the history of the American military and one of the greatest victories ever won by a Native American force.

Ironically, the death of Custer and all of his men was seen as a heroic event in the East. Artists painted hundreds of pictures showing Custer's bravery and glory, and Custer is still thought of as a great hero today.

"Custer's Last Stand," one of the greatest disasters in the history of the American military, has been remembered by some Americans as a heroic event.

The Ghost Dance and the Battle of Wounded Knee

He was a shaman (SHAW-mun), or holy man, of the Paiute (PIE-yoot) tribe, and he had a vision of a world where Native Americans lived in peace and prosperity. In his dream, the white people would disappear and the Native Americans would be reborn into a new world—a world where their land, the buffalo they hunted, and the friends they had lost in battle would be restored to them.

The shaman's name was Wovoka (woh-VOH-kuh), and he taught a ceremonial dance that he said would help make his vision a reality. The dance, known to white people as the "Ghost Dance," gave new hope to Native Americans who had been driven off their lands and were living on reservations. U.S. military personnel who witnessed the Ghost Dances did not know what they meant and viewed the rituals with great suspicion.

Many of the Native Americans who participated in the dances wore shirts marked with magic designs that they felt would protect them from bullets, in case U.S. soldiers attacked. The soldiers could not understand why the dancers wore these shirts. They assumed the shirts were uniforms and that the dancers were planning an attack. This only served to increase suspicion and tension.

Fearing the Ghost Dance frenzy that was sweeping through Native American reservations throughout the West, the U.S. Army sent troops to the Pine Ridge Reservation in South Dakota in the fall of 1890. There they arrested the famous Hunkpapa Sioux warrior and medicine man Sitting Bull.

Sitting Bull was not in favor of the Ghost Dance, but he had done nothing to stop the ceremonies. The Army arrested him because it believed he had started the Ghost Dance and was encouraging unrest.

When the soldiers came to arrest Sitting Bull, a group of Native Americans tried to rescue him. There was a scuffle, and shots were fired. Six of the army officers and six of the Native Americans were killed. Sitting Bull was one of them.

A dancer performing the ceremonial "Ghost Dance" that was meant to bring
freedom, peace, and prosperity to Native Americans.

Reacting to the killing, hundreds of Native Americans ran away from the reservations. Chief Big Foot of the Miniconjou (mih-neh-KAHN-joo) Sioux led his people to a site called Wounded Knee.

There, the cavalry caught up with them and ordered them to give up their guns.

No one is certain of what happened next. Some of the Sioux refused to surrender their weapons. While soldiers searched their teepees for guns, somebody fired a shot. The soldiers reacted by shooting at the Sioux, killing nearly three hundred people, including women and children.

The Sioux were forced to surrender to the more than 3,000 U.S. soldiers confronting them. The tragic massacre at Wounded Knee not only killed many Native Americans, but also killed their hopes and dreams of one day living again as a free people.

A Sioux warrior visiting the burial site of one of his comrades who died at Wounded Knee.

KAITCHKNOA

The wars between the United States and Native American nations produced many individual heroes and victims for both sides. One woman whose role often has been overlooked by historians was Kaitchknoa, a member of the Modoc tribe that lived along the California-Oregon border.

Kaitchknoa was well known for her acts of bravery fighting alongside her people's warriors in battle, and for shooting a large grizzly bear. She also served as an interpreter between the United States military and the Modocs during the "Indian Wars." Her great skill in this role helped reduce tensions between the U.S. forces and the Modocs. When she learned of a Modoc plot to kill U.S. army officers, she chose to warn them. Although it meant betraying her tribe, she felt the move was necessary to prevent the senseless bloodshed and the acts of revenge that would surely be taken against her people. Unfortunately, Kaitchknoa's warning was not taken seriously, and the army officers were killed. Nonetheless, her decision was a great act of bravery that put her at considerable risk, and she deserves to be remembered among the heroes of the tragic wars between the United States and Native Americans.

The Modoc woman Kaitchknoa was famous for her acts of bravery,
such as shooting a large grizzly bear.

ELIZABETH FITZPATRICK CLIFTON

Some western women are remembered more for what they endured than for what they accomplished. Women living in wilderness lands suffered great hardships. They were isolated from friends and family, and did their best when confronted with unsanitary living conditions. And there were sometimes raids by Native American tribes, who might capture and enslave women settlers.

What happened to Elizabeth Fitzpatrick Clifton was an example of the terror some women of the West would experience at the hands of Native Americans during the "Indian Wars." When her cabin in Texas was attacked by nearly one thousand Kiowa and Comanche warriors, Elizabeth and members of her family fired their guns at the attackers. The warriors broke down the door of the cabin, and Clifton was forced to watch as her daughter was killed.

Clifton and her thirteen-year-old son Joseph were taken as slaves by the raiders. During their journey to the Native American camp, Joseph was placed on a pile of brush and burned. Once again, Clifton was forced to witness the death of her child.

Life in the camp meant more suffering. Clifton lived on a diet of raw liver and dog meat, and was repeatedly beaten by her captors.

Clifton was finally rescued after spending more than a year as a slave in the camp. Stories of her suffering motivated U.S. Army officers to intensify their search for other possible captives of Native American tribes.

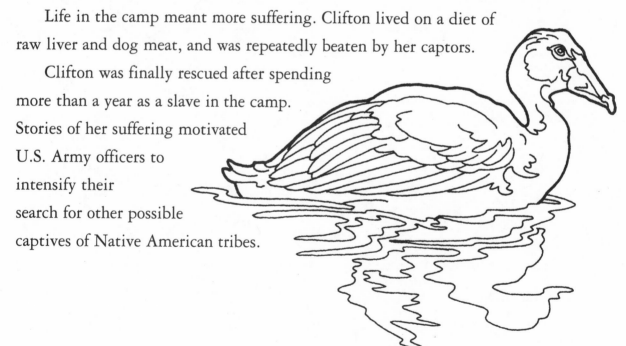

Settler Elizabeth Fitzpatrick Clifton spent more than a year as a slave in a Native American camp.

PART 6

Law and Lawlessness in the Wild West

Lawlessness was a part of many frontier settlements in the West. With all the money around, con artists, thieves, pickpockets, cattle rustlers, and train robbers flocked to mining camps, cow towns, and boom towns, where they hoped to take advantage of innocent people.

Law enforcement authorities in these areas were often weak, ineffective, and unprepared for the criminals. Some lawmen were dishonest and criminal themselves. To law-abiding citizens, the only way to keep order seemed to be by taking the law into their own hands.

In San Francisco, where the population jumped from 800 in 1848 to nearly 55,000 in 1855, residents began forming "Committees of Vigilance" to catch and punish criminals. The committees, whose membership was not secret, quickly began to bring justice to the city, punishing criminals by whipping them, hanging them, or banishing them from town.

Similar committees were formed in other western towns, and although criminals continued to come in search of easy money, the murder rate began to drop and law and order began to replace violence and thievery.

The committees of vigilance were not always fair in the way they dispensed justice, and eventually they were forced to break up as stronger, more official law enforcement agencies came to the West.

The legacy of the committees survives today. Ever since the first Committee of Vigilance was formed in San Francisco in 1851, private citizens who decide to take law enforcement into their own hands have been known as *vigilantes* (vi-juh-LAN-tees).

Members of a Committee of Vigilance—private citizens who took the law into their own hands—
sometimes turned criminals over to town peace officers.

THE JAMES-YOUNGER GANG

One day in 1866, an unknown group of young men held up a bank in Liberty, Missouri, and made off with $60,000. It was the beginning of a string of robberies that would bring huge amounts of loot—and an almost heroic fame—to two of the most dastardly outlaws of the Old West: Jesse James and his brother Frank.

Jesse and Frank had been soldiers in the Confederate Army during the Civil War. Unhappy with the victory of the Union forces and still thirsty for fighting, they embarked on a life of crime after the Confederate Army surrendered.

The James Brothers joined up with the Younger Brothers—Bob, Cole, and Jim—not long after. Together, they set out on a long chain of bank, train, stagecoach, and steamboat robberies. Over the years, the James-Younger gang stole almost $500,000 in loot, and killed nearly thirty men throughout the Southwest.

Sometimes the gang made raids into northern lands. One such raid brought an end to the gang in 1876, when they tried to stage a robbery in Northfield, Minnesota. A group of private citizens stood up to the bandits, and a shootout took place as they tried to escape.

All three of the Younger brothers were captured. Bob died in prison in 1889, and Cole and Jim spent twenty-five years in jail. The James brothers got away and laid low for a while, but then went back to a life of crime.

Then, in the 1880s, Missouri Governor Thomas Crittenden hired a former member of the James gang, Robert Ford, to hunt down and kill Jesse. Ford visited Jesse at his home and shot him in the back, putting an end to Jesse's legendary life of crime.

Members of the notorious James-Younger gang, preparing to rob a train.

CATTLE RUSTLERS

As cow towns sprung up across the great western plains in the 1860s and 1870s, they attracted plenty of dishonest people looking for easy money. Towns such as Abilene, Deadwood, Tombstone, and Dodge City attracted so much crime and violence that they became known as "bad towns."

Among the criminals who came to these towns were cattle thieves, also known as *cattle rustlers*. The great herds of cattle grazing on the vast grasslands were an open invitation to the rustlers. Small groups of cows who strayed from the herd in search of water or better grazing were easy prey.

When rustlers took cows from a herd, their first task was to change the legitimate owner's *brand* so the cows could not be identified as stolen. The brand was a mark burned into the cows' hide with a hot iron. Each cattle owner had a specific brand that identified his cows.

To change the brand, rustlers had to burn a new mark into the cows' hide, but since branding irons were large and difficult to hide, the rustlers resorted to a variety of smaller devices. They heated anything from horseshoes and belt buckles to telegraph wires to burn a new mark into the cows they stole.

Rustlers often sought to separate new-born calves from their mothers. Since the calves had not yet been branded, they could be claimed more easily by the thieves. To separate the calves from their mothers, the rustlers would cut the calves' tongues to prevent them from nursing, or damage one of their eyes so they couldn't see well. This would cause the calves to wander away from the herd, away from the watchful eyes of the cowboys. Then the rustlers could make off with them.

Law enforcement officers were unable to bring an end to cattle rustling—most cow towns had only a token *peace officer* charged with keeping order. But the invention of barbed wire fencing in the 1890s did provide a solution to the problem. With barbed wire, cattlemen could fence in their grazing lands and keep their cattle from wandering over the open range, where they could fall victim to cattle rustlers.

Rustlers attempted to drive herds of cattle to stampede, hoping
to separate and steal some of the cows.

The Gunfight at the OK Corral

"Murdered in the streets of Tombstone" is written on the headstones of three graves at the Boot Hill Cemetery in Tombstone, Arizona. The Wild West was full of stories about show-downs between lawmen and outlaws, but perhaps none has taken on such mythic proportions as the "Gunfight at the OK Corral."

Billy Clanton, Tom McLaury, and Frank McLaury—three trouble-making cattle rustlers—lost their lives on October 26, 1881, when a feud between them the Earp brothers escalated to an all-out gunfight.

Wyatt Earp was Tombstone's peace officer, and his brother Virgil served as his deputy. Although the Earps represented the law, they were involved in many corrupt activities. Wyatt, Virgil, their brother Morgan, and Doc Holliday—the town dentist—had been accused of murder and robbery by Clanton and the McLaurys.

Angered by the accusations, the Earps and Doc Holliday tried several times to provoke a gunfight with Clanton and the McLaurys. Virgil Earp had beaten up Clanton for carrying a weapon within the city limits. Wyatt Earp also beat up one of the McLaurys, who tried to help Clanton when he was arrested and taken to court. The feud between the two groups had reached the boiling point, and each group vowed to kill the other on sight.

The gunfight occurred when the Earps and Doc Holliday met Clanton and his friends outside the OK Corral in Tombstone. When the shooting ended, Clanton and his friends were dead, and Virgil and Morgan Earp were wounded.

None of the players in this violent scene was a law-abiding citizen. Clanton and his companions were involved in several robberies and cattle rustling. Doc Holliday was believed to have robbed stagecoaches and to have committed several murders. Wyatt Earp was a gambler, swindler, and horse thief. It is Wyatt, however, who is remembered as the hero of the famous gunfight at the OK Corral.

The Earp brothers and Doc Holliday, preparing for a showdown at the OK Corral.

Butch Cassidy and the Sundance Kid

A narrow gap in a steep red sandstone cliff was the entrance to a hideout for murderers, bandits, train robbers, and cattle rustlers. Known as the "Hole-in-the-Wall," this natural stone formation sheltered some of the roughest criminal gangs that roamed the territories of Wyoming, Colorado, Montana, and Utah.

Two of the most famous outlaws to occupy the Hole-in-the-Wall hideout were Robert Leroy Parker and Harry Longbaugh—otherwise known as Butch Cassidy and the Sundance Kid. Parker had changed his name to Cassidy in honor of the man who had taught him the art of cattle rustling. Longbaugh had been in prison in Sundance, Wyoming, and took his name from the town.

These two men became the leaders of an outlaw gang known as the "Wild Bunch" that cleverly pulled off dozens of crimes in the 1890s. The Wild Bunch planned everything down to the last detail. They knew the territory well enough to escape from the *posses* (PAW-seez)—groups of armed men—that chased after them. They kept fresh horses waiting at key points along their escape route back to the Hole-in-the-Wall.

The Wild Bunch began as cattle rustlers, but eventually gave up rustling in favor of more profitable train robberies and bank hold-ups. Butch Cassidy and the Sundance Kid were so successful that word of their escapades traveled throughout the country. Nearly one hundred outlaws came to join their gang.

One of their heists, in which they robbed a coal company, produced a take of $9,000. The Wild Bunch once also robbed the Union Pacific Railroad of $30,000.

Railroads and banks throughout the West insisted that the Wild Bunch be stopped and punished, and lawmen finally began catching up with some members of the gang.

With the law closing in on them, Butch Cassidy and the Sundance Kid staged a few last robberies—enough to give them the money they needed to escape to South America. Not long after their arrival in Bolivia, the pair began a new life of crime. No one is sure what finally became of them, but it is believed they were killed by the Bolivian army. Their daring life of crime turned Butch Cassidy and the Sundance Kid into legendary villains of the Wild West, and their adventures still thrill us today.

Members of Butch Cassidy's Wild Bunch made their hideout in the "Hole-in-the-Wall."

THE RANGE WARS

Violence and bloodshed also came to the great western plains in the form of wars between cattlemen and sheepherders.

Cowboys working for cattle ranchers quickly came to dislike sheepherders, who walked the grazing lands with their flocks and their dogs. The cowboys felt that the sheep chewed the grass too short, leaving nothing for the cattle. They became angry when the sheep's hooves tore up the grasslands. In truth, the sheep ate grasses that the cattle would not eat. They also ate weeds that choked the grasses, and their droppings acted as fertilizer. But cowboys refused to believe these arguments when they heard them from the sheepherders, and they became determined to eliminate the sheep.

Violence against the sheep and their owners developed quickly. Cattlemen burned the homes of sheepherders and slaughtered their flocks. They drove the sheep to stampede. They even used dynamite to blow up the flocks! Cattlemen ordered the sheepherders to leave their homes and campsites, but the sheepherders often refused. There were terrible fights, and men and animals were killed. One sheepherder who had paid $1,000 for each of a special species of ram watched as cowboys killed his valued flock.

The range wars—so called because they were fought on the open range—took place from Texas to Colorado, and as far north as Idaho and Oregon. The violence continued through the last half of the nineteenth century, and even into the early twentieth century.

The cattlemen eventually realized that sheep could be beneficial to cattle grazing. They brought sheep into their cattle herds, and the range wars came to a close.

A masked cowboy, trying to drive sheepherders off their land, flees after setting fire to their home.

THE FENCE-CUTTER WARS

Our history books say little or nothing about barbed wire. In the 1890s, the introduction of barbed wire as fencing for cattle grazing lands brought many changes to life in the West.

As wealthy cattle ranchers put up barbed-wire fencing to keep their cattle from straying, problems arose for homesteaders and cattlemen who owned smaller herds. The barbed-wire fences denied homesteaders and the owners of small cattle herds access to watering holes and public roads. They protested the fencing, but the politicians and wealthy ranchers refused to listen. More and more barbed-wire fences went up.

For those who were shut out by the wealthy cattlemen, the solution was to cut the fences and burn the wooden posts that held the barbed wire in place. Secret groups worked through the night cutting fences, burning grazing lands, and destroying thousands of dollars worth of property.

As the activities escalated, cattlemen shot at fence cutters who damaged their fences. The fence cutters threatened the cattlemen, sometimes forcing them to sell their ranches and flee for their lives. Cattlemen responded by spreading rumors that bombs had been planted in the fence posts. This frightened the fence cutters, who began to cut back their activities. As the violence of the fence-cutter wars increased, politicians began to take an interest in stopping the vandalism and bloodshed. Laws were passed to punish fence cutters with prison terms; other laws prohibited unlawful fencing. The fence-cutter wars ended in victory for both cattle ranchers and fence cutters.

A fence cutter preparing to dismantle the barbed-wire fence of a prosperous cattle rancher.

PEARL HART

Pearl Hart was known nationwide as the last stagecoach bandit in the American West.

Hart had fallen on hard times when she married a man who beat her. She also became addicted to opium from a medicine she took for an illness. Forced into poverty, she took work as a cook in an Arizona mining camp. There she met a miner named John Boot who convinced her to help him in the robbery of a stagecoach. At the time, stagecoach travel was quickly being replaced by train travel, and there were few coaches left.

When the robbery took place, the stagecoach passengers were shocked to discover that one of the thieves was a woman. Hart took more than $400 from the passengers before she and Boot rode off into some rough country in search of a hideout.

Before long, she and her accomplice were arrested. Both were tried in court by a jury that found them guilty and sent them to prison. Boot served thirty-five years; Hart served five.

As a result of her daring stagecoach robbery, Pearl Hart had become famous. She tried to take advantage of her new celebrity status by portraying her life in a stage play. When the play failed, she joined Buffalo Bill's Wild West Show. She was last seen in 1957 on the streets of Tucson, Arizona. Pearl Hart's fame as the last stagecoach robber guaranteed her a place in the history of the West.

Pearl Heart stopping a stagecoach, for what turned out to be the last stagecoach robbery in the American West.

PART 7

Great Figures and Legends of the West

Books, movies, and television shows have given us distorted images of what life was like in the "Old West." Many unworthy individuals have been portrayed as dashing heroes, and many western lifestyles that were in reality hard and thankless have been shown as glamorous.

The life of the cowboy has been glorified as action-packed, heroic, and adventuresome. Actually, the cowboy was a hired worker who usually did not own his own horse. He was a cow herder, not a gunfighter. In fact, most cowboys rarely carried guns.

Wyatt Earp gained fame as a heroic lawman at the OK Coral. But Earp was a lawman who did not always stay on the right side of the law. He owned the biggest gambling house in Tombstone, Arizona, and some historians think he was also a horse thief and cattle rustler.

Wild Bill Hickok was hired as Marshall to bring justice to the corrupt city of Abilene, Kansas. But instead of living up to his sworn duty, Hickok took bribes from gamblers and refused to put a stop to illegal activities in the town. He was shot while gambling and was buried in Deadwood, South Dakota. People who still see him as a hero visit his grave each year.

In the town of Lincoln, New Mexico, the memory of Billy the Kid is celebrated each year in a special pageant. The jail break in which the legendary outlaw killed two deputy sheriffs is reenacted in the pageant. In fact, Billy the Kid was a ruthless killer whose exploits had no real impact on the history of the West. The legends about his life have grown over the years, turning him into a heroic figure—a sort of Robin Hood of the West.

As we learn more about the famous people of the American West, their real lives turn out to be much different than the picture sometimes presented to us. Perhaps it will take a long time before we know the truth about some of the individuals who played important roles in the Old West.

Life in the Old West has been glorified in books, movies, and television shows.

THE LEGEND OF PECOS BILL

The Old West was indeed a place of hardship and adventure. Tales of the people who lived there have been blown up into wild legends in today's society. Many tall tales were also told by the people who lived in the Old West. One of the most popular of these myths was the legend of Pecos Bill, the King of the Cowboys.

When Bill was just a baby, folks said, he wanted a teddy bear. Since he couldn't find one, he climbed out of his crib one day and went into the wilderness. There he caught himself a grizzly bear for a pet!

Later, when Bill and his parents moved out West, he supposedly bounced out of the covered wagon, got lost, and was raised by coyotes. For years he thought he was a coyote, until a cowboy saw him drinking water out of the Pecos River in Texas and told him he was human. That's where he got the name Pecos Bill.

Pecos Bill went off with his new friend to become a cowboy. According to the story, they were attacked by a mountain lion on the way, but Bill wrestled it to the ground and rode it all the way back to camp.

When a ten-foot-long rattlesnake sprang at them, Bill grabbed it by the tail and swung it around and around his head. The spinning made the snake stretch out until it was very thin and thirty feet long. Bill later used his snake-rope to lasso a cow. That's how cattle roping was invented, they say.

According to this tall tale, Pecos Bill eventually settled down and got married to a woman named Slue-foot Sue. Sue was known to ride on the back of a whale in the Rio Grande River, the story goes, and was once thrown all the way to the moon by a bucking bronco!

Stories of the adventures of Pecos Bill and Slue-foot Sue can amuse us, but they have no basis in reality. On the pages that follow, you'll read about some of the great personalities of the West whose true-life accomplishments still thrill us today.

Pecos Bill wrestling a mountain lion near the Rio Grande River.

BUFFALO BILL

He brought the West to the East. His shows presented the great drama of the raw American West to audiences in the Eastern United States and Europe. More than five hundred books were written about him, making Buffalo Bill Cody a legend in his own lifetime. More than any other western personality, he captured the public's imagination with his incredible deeds and the adventures he depicted in his famous Wild West Shows.

William F. Cody was known as Buffalo Bill because he killed more than four thousand buffalo and sold the meat to railroad workers who were building tracks through the West. At the age of fifteen, he joined the Pony Express and set new records for speed and distance. Once, after his usual run on the Pony Express route, Buffalo Bill discovered that the members of his relief stations had been killed in raids by Native Americans. He continued his ride for a total of 322 miles, one of the longest rides in the brief history of the Pony Express.

Like many of the stories in Buffalo Bill's life, solid historical facts are hard to find. He claims to have killed Chief Yellow Hand, a Cheyenne, in hand-to-hand combat. The story has never been confirmed, but it was often played out as one of the acts in Buffalo Bill's Wild West Show. It is known that Bill Cody served as a military scout and as a volunteer in a cavalry group known as Jennison's Jayhawkers.

Perhaps Buffalo Bill's most important role was as the founder of a theatrical company that brought the scenes of the American West to the folks back east. Among the members of his famous cast were "Little Sure Shot" Annie Oakley and Chief Sitting Bull. Bill also employed sixteen Rough Riders—soldiers who gained fame for their exploits in the Spanish-American War. In his show, they re-enacted their famous charge at the Battle of San Juan Hill. Regular tours of the show were taken to England and France, where the drama of the American West provided excitement for European audiences.

Buffalo Bill Cody died in 1917 at the age of seventy. Today he lies buried at Lookout Mountain in Colorado. No other personality created a more exciting view of the American West.

Buffalo Bill demonstrating his sharp shooting skills in a Wild West Show.

ANNIE OAKLEY

Chief Sitting Bull named her "Little Sure Shot," and her name was known to most Americans and many Europeans. She was invited to visit Queen Victoria, who spoke of her as being a "clever little girl." Her dressing rooms were always filled with flowers from her many admirers. Annie Oakley had become world famous during her days of performing in Buffalo Bill's Wild West Shows.

Born August 13, 1860, Annie Oakley had a difficult childhood. When her father died, hard times fell upon her family. She found work at an early age, caring for children at an infirmary.

As a young girl, Annie frequently hunted, shooting game with her father's rifle. She sold much of what she shot to tavern owners. The tavern owners were pleasantly surprised to find that the animals they bought had no gunshot lead in their bodies. Annie had such good aim that all of the pheasants, rabbits, and turkeys she sold had been shot in the head!

Her marksmanship brought Annie into competitions at gun clubs and special events. She amazed the audiences with her sharp-shooting tricks. She would throw five balls into the air and break them all with rifle shots in five seconds. She would also shoot holes in admission tickets at events. Since free tickets had holes punched in them to distinguish them from paid tickets, free tickets soon became known as "Annie Oakleys."

Annie met her future husband, Frank Butler, when she defeated him in a rifle shooting match. They married in 1876, when Annie was sixteen years old. Their marriage lasted fifty years.

Annie's special talents were recognized by Buffalo Bill, who saw a place for her in his Wild West Show. It was during her long run with the show that Annie gained an international reputation as an extraordinary sharpshooter. At a time when the United States had not yet given women the right to vote, Annie demonstrated that she could do better than a man in a man's sport. She was an inspiration to many young women of her generation.

"Little Sure Shot" Annie Oakley taking aim.

CALAMITY JANE

No one knows for sure how Calamity Jane got her nickname. Some say she was called "Calamity" because she had so much hard luck, others say it's because she was always helping out victims of disasters.

Born in Missouri around 1852, Martha Jane Canary later moved west with her parents. They joined a wagon train to Montana. By the time she was fifteen years old, Jane had lost both of her parents, and she began her life as a rough and ready wanderer. Often dressed in men's clothing, Jane followed along with Union Pacific crews as they built the transcontinental railroad. She also served as a soldier, worked as a prospector, and gave distinguished service as a nurse.

Jane was in Wyoming in 1875. Posing as a man, she signed on as one of four hundred soldiers escorting a geological expedition from Fort Laramie into the Black Hills. Not long after, an officer discovered she was a woman and drove her out of the unit.

She followed the gold rush to Deadwood, South Dakota, in 1876. There she met and became friends with Wild Bill Hickok, the famous scout and frontier marshall. In 1878, a smallpox epidemic broke out in Deadwood. Jane served as a nurse, living with and caring for patients who were quarantined in a crude log cabin pesthouse.

After the mining boom ended in Deadwood, Jane went back to roaming about the West. She met a man named Clinton Burke in El Paso, Texas, and married him in 1891. Their marriage did not last long, however, and Jane soon went back to her shiftless wanderings, drifting from town to town and selling a small leaflet about her life.

Calamity Jane died in Terry, South Dakota, in 1903. Tourists can still visit her grave in nearby Deadwood.

Some folks say Martha Jane Canary was known as "Calamity Jane" because she had such a rough
life; others say it's because she helped disaster victims.

ARTISTS OF THE WEST

Before photography equipment became publicly available in 1839, paintings and drawings by artists provided the only visual records of life on the American frontier. Even after the advent of photographs, however, artists continued to portray the West. These artists have left us an important and stunning record of western life.

George Catlin

George Catlin was a young, self-trained artist who wanted to record the life of Native Americans before their civilization disappeared. In 1830, Catlin gave up a career as a Pennsylvania lawyer to travel through the West and observe Native American culture firsthand. There, his paintings brought to life the character, activities, and ceremonies of the Native American way of life. Catlin's painting of a Mandan buffalo dance is one of the best representations we have of this ceremony.

Today, most of the nearly 600 paintings completed by Catlin are on display in the Smithsonian Institution in Washington, D.C.

Karl Bodmer

Karl Bodmer was a Swiss artist who traveled up the Missouri River into Montana in 1833. Helped by fur trappers who knew Native American languages, Bodmer was able to contact many tribes and paint portraits of their members.

Bodmer's portrait of a six-foot-tall warrior is one of the best early records of a Native American style of dress. The painting shows a young man dressed in a beaded buffalo robe and wearing a bear-claw necklace. He holds an eagle-wing fan in his hand, and wolves' tails are attached to his brightly decorated moccasins.

Bodmer was another artist whose fine works have preserved for us details of life in the wilderness before the invention of photography.

Mandan dancers preparing for a buffalo dance, as George Catlin paints their camp.

Frederic Remington

Frederic Remington was one of the most important artists of the American West. His drawings, paintings, and sculpture give us a spectacular view of the Native Americans, cowboys, ranchers, fur trappers, and animals that populated the western territories in the late nineteenth century.

One of Remington's favorite subjects was that of cowboys riding untamed horses. His works capture the action of men roping horses or being thrown from bucking broncos. The horses' muscles and the tense expressions on the cowboys' faces stand out in vivid detail. One of Remington's most famous bronze sculptures shows a horse startled by a rattlesnake, and the expression of utter surprise on the rider's face.

Remington also created many works depicting Native Americans. One bronze sculpture shows a Cheyenne warrior galloping fiercely on horseback with a spear in his hand. The sculpture shows the determination of the Native American to defend his way of life. In another work, a painting called "The Buffalo Hunt," we see the drama of Native American hunters, spears in hand, chasing after a herd of buffalo. A fallen horse, injured by buffalo horns, lies in the background.

In another of Remington's bronze sculptures, four cowboys gallop into town on a Saturday night. As a sign that they have no violent intentions, they fire their pistols in the air, emptying their guns before arriving at the saloon.

Remington, who lived from 1861 to 1909, spent much of his life in the East, but he took frequent trips to the West to gather information and inspiration for his work. The artifacts he collected on his journeys enabled him to portray western life with great style and accuracy.

People all over the country knew of Remington's work during his lifetime. He became famous by publishing his pictures in popular magazines. Through his illustrations, Easterners were able to form an idea of what life was like in the West. His paintings, drawings, and sculptures serve a similar purpose for us today.

Frederic Remington's "The Cowboy," painted in 1902.

Charles Marion Russell

Another great painter and sculptor of the American West was Charles Marion Russell, a Missouri-born cowboy.

Russell's works are one of our best sources for studying Native American clothing and beadwork. His paintings of some Native Americans are so detailed that it is possible to identify what tribe they belonged to just by looking at their clothes. Details revealed in his painting of a cowboy on horseback could be used to tell where the cowboy bought his saddle. Because they are so accurate, his sculptures are a valuable resource for naturalists who study different types of animals.

The subjects Russell chose to paint tell much about the life of both the Native American and the cowboy. We see scenes of Native Americans scraping and preparing buffalo hides. In one extraordinary picture, Russell shows us a Native American riding his horse at great speed as he attempts to kill a buffalo with a bow and arrow. In another painting, he shows us a cowboy shooting a buffalo with a rifle.

Russell's art presents us with many exciting scenes of life in the West during the last quarter of the nineteenth century. Some of his works are humorous, such as one in which a horse kicks about wildly, knocking over pots and pans as he backs into the chuckwagon at a cowboy camp. Other scenes are more serious, depicting attacks against fur trappers and scenes of combat. Some paintings show Native Americans performing war dances or stopping wagon trains to ask for bribes that would guarantee the pioneers safe passage along the trail.

Russell was fascinated by the journals of Lewis and Clark that describe their epic journey through the West. After reading the journals, he painted scenes from the expedition. One such scene shows Lewis and Clark meeting the Chinook tribe of Native Americans on the Lower Columbia River. Sacajawea is also seen in the picture, acting as interpreter.

For both historians and the public, the paintings, drawings, and sculpture of Charles Marion Russell are a valuable record of the lives of typical western settlers, ranchers, cowboys, and Native Americans.

A detail from Charles Marion Russell's "Buffalo Hunting," painted in 1894.

John Gutzon Borglum

Hundreds of small dynamite explosions carved the heads of four United States presidents in the side of South Dakota's Mount Rushmore. The sixty-foot-tall faces of George Washington, Thomas Jefferson, Abraham Lincoln, and Theodore Roosevelt are an impressive sight.

John Gutzon Borglum, the sculptor who created the faces, had a great vision for a monument that would capture the spirit of America. He wanted to carve the heads of four presidents who had a special role in the building of the United States: Washington, who founded the nation; Lincoln, who held it together through the Civil War; Jefferson, who purchased the Louisiana Territory and expanded America westward; and Roosevelt, who protected the rights of the working man.

To carve the mountain, Borglum first made models in his studio. A large window in the studio looked out over the face of Mount Rushmore, where the four presidents' heads would be carved. The work began in 1927. Money for the project was always in short supply. School children, civic organizations, and some large corporations contributed funds, but they were never enough. Finally, the federal government provided money to continue the work.

The workers who came from nearby towns had a steep climb to get to the top of the work site. Hanging in chairs suspended from the heads they were carving, they used steel drills to cut holes into the granite surface of the mountain. Small charges of dynamite were placed in the drilled holes and then blown up. Although there were many dangers, no workman was killed or injured seriously.

The work was completed by 1941, and Borglum's dream of creating a great shrine to democracy became a reality. Today, thousands of visitors who come to see this monumental work stand in awe of Borglum's vision.

It took workers fourteen years, from 1927 to 1941, to carve the heads of four presidents into the face of Mount Rushmore.

JOHN LORENZO HUBBELL AND HARRY GOULDING

In 1870, John Lorenzo Hubbell opened a trading post on the Navajo Reservation in Arizona in hopes of encouraging better relationships between the Navajo people and white settlers.

Hubbell was successful in helping the Navajo people. When a smallpox epidemic hit the reservation in 1886, he gave them aid and medical supplies. His trading post provided a market where they could sell their hand-woven rugs, pottery, jewelry, and baskets. This allowed them to earn better livings. Hubbell also employed the Navajo as clerks in the trading post.

Hubbell's trading post is operated today by the National Park Service. Visitors also may tour Hubbell's home. There they can see some of the most beautiful rugs, jewelry, and pottery created by Navajo craftsmen. The trading post still sells the arts and crafts of the Zuni, Hopi, and Navajo tribes. It also offers demonstrations of traditional jewelry making and basket and rug weaving techniques.

Another important trading post was founded in Monument Valley, Utah, by Harry Goulding after the first World War. Goulding came to Monument Valley in the early 1920's after his discharge from the military.

Like Hubbell, Goulding was saddened by the poverty and hardships of the local Native Americans, and he became good friends with them. He, too, offered them jobs and a place to sell their goods.

During the Great Depression of 1930, when jobs were extremely scarce, especially for Native Americans, Goulding traveled to Hollywood to see if he could interest people in coming to Monument Valley to make movies. He convinced director John Ford to bring his studio to Utah to make the John Wayne film "Stagecoach." The film, which won the Academy Award for Best Picture, employed many Native Americans in its battle scenes. The actors were paid five dollars extra if they fell off their horses when another actor shot at them. As a result, it was not uncommon to see as many as six Native American actors fall off their horses in response to only one of John Wayne's bullets!

Western trading posts sold everything from basic supplies to rugs, pottery, and jewelry.

PART 8

National Parks and Monuments of the West

Boiling mud pots, slow-moving glaciers, sculptured pink and white monuments of stone, and deep gorges carved by mountain streams are some of the extraordinary features of our magnificent American West.

Some of the early visitors to the magnificent western mountains, rivers, lakes, forests, and valleys felt the need to preserve these wonderlands of nature. National parks, which are established by the U.S. Congress, and national monuments, which are created by U.S. presidents, are areas that have been set aside to protect them from logging and mining companies that wanted to exploit their natural resources.

National parks and monuments also protect archaeological sites. The prehistoric inhabitants of our continent left evidence of their existence in the form of great buildings, pottery, tools, and other artifacts. Before the federal government protected the sites where such evidence was found, thieves and looters—sometimes called "pot hunters"—often dug up Native American artifacts and sold them for profit. When these archaeological sites came under the protection of the National Park Service, the fragile remnants of past societies were carefully preserved.

The Park Service's policy is to keep Native American sites in their present condition by repairing them when needed, but not restoring them to what they may have looked like when they were inhabited. When visiting a National Park where there are archaeological sites, such as Mesa Verde or Chaco Canyon, you can be sure that the ruins you see have been left just as they were found.

The National Park system was designed to protect our country's natural and archaeological heritage from industrial exploitation and destruction, but parks and monuments throughout the West now face a new danger: too many visitors. Millions of tourists visiting the parks each year strain the camping facilities and road systems. The exhaust from their thousands of automobiles pollutes the environment and takes its toll on many fragile and unique life forms.

The natural beauty of western parks and monuments has attracted thousands of visitors.

YELLOWSTONE NATIONAL PARK

It was known as Colter's Hell. John Colter, probably the first white man to visit Yellowstone, described fantastic geysers spouting water high into the air, boiling mud pots, rivers of steaming hot water running through the countryside, and strange terraces of limestone.

The Yellowstone Basin was created in one of the most powerful explosions that ever shook the earth. More than a half million years ago, lava from a huge volcano rushed out of the ground and covered a wide area of western Wyoming. As the lava poured forth, the inside of the volcano emptied and eventually collapsed in on itself, creating a huge crater.

Today this region is known as Yellowstone National Park. In 1872, after several scientific expeditions had confirmed Colter's observations, it became the first national park in the United States.

Geysers form some of the most interesting sights at Yellowstone National Park. Water seeping into the earth reaches areas underground that are still very hot from volcanic forces. The extreme heat turns the water into steam and forces it to spout out of the earth as a geyser. The best known geyser in Yellowstone is unquestionably "Old Faithful." Erupting approximately twenty times a day, with water spouts that reach a height of sixty feet or more, Old Faithful has become one of the park's major attractions.

There are a number of other sites in Yellowstone that have geyser basins. These basins have brightly colored pools of water of many different temperatures and colors. The pools are inhabited by a wide variety of algae, which take on different colors depending on the temperature of the water.

At Yellowstone's Mammouth Hot Springs, lime-rich waters cascade down the mountainside to form step-like terraces that hold the pools of water. The colored pools and shapes of the terraces are one more spectacular sight in this volcanic wonderland that has been preserved for all Americans by the National Park Service.

The eruptions of Old Faithful can spout water as high as sixty feet.

DEVIL'S TOWER

Rising 867 feet out of the ground, with an acre and a half of grassy fields at its top, the mysterious stone formation known as *Devil's Tower* has attracted thousands of visitors and rock climbers over the last century.

Devil's Tower was established as the country's first national monument in 1906 by President Theodore Roosevelt. It is a rock formation shaped like an enormous tree trunk growing out of the western end of the Black Hills in northeast Wyoming.

The tower was formed around sixty million years ago, at a time when the dinosaurs who once ruled the earth were dying out. This was also the time when the Rocky Mountains were rising out of the earth.

During the upheaval, enormous pressures forced great masses of molten rock up through the soft layers of the earth's outer crust. The molten rock cooled as it rose and hardened into unusual stone formations buried beneath the ground. Over the millennia that followed, the softer layers of earth were eroded away by nature's elements, leaving the harder stone shapes standing naked and alone above the landscape.

This is the scientific explanation for how Devil's Tower was formed. But Kiowa Native Americans living near the solitary tower explained it in another way. OneKiowa story explains both the formation of Devil's Tower and the origins of the constellation we call the "Pleiades."

One day, the story goes, seven girls were being chased by bears. They escaped by jumping onto a rock that rose suddenly up from the ground, lifting them beyond the reach of the pursuing grizzlies. As the bears scratched at the rock, the girls were lifted up into the heavens, where they became the seven stars of the constellation. This story also explains why the layers of stone on the sides of Devil's Tower look like they have been scraped by giant claws—they are the scratch marks of the bears that chased the seven girls.

Devil's Tower has intrigued Americans for more than a hundred years. It was first climbed in 1893, and now thousands of people have scaled its walls to reach the grassy field at the top.

Devil's Tower in Wyoming looks like it has been clawed by bears, according to a Kiowa legend.

GLACIER NATIONAL PARK

In northwestern Montana, visitors can find a scenic wonderland sculpted by the forces of nature. Glacier National Park formed millions of years ago when waters covering the region retreated and left the land mass exposed. Later, glaciers sweeping across the area carved the landscape into the deep valleys that may be seen throughout the park today.

Great pressures from within the earth opened a huge crack that split the land mass at Glacier National Park and sent the rock on one side of the crack sliding over the rock on the other side. Today, this unusual stone formation is known as the "Lewis Overthrust."

As glaciers melted over the centuries, running streams cut more valleys through the landscape and formed huge lakes that sparkle today throughout the park. Most of the glaciers melted away four thousand years ago, but a number of these giant sheets of ice and snow still exist in the park.

The Continental Divide runs through Glacier National Park, separating the eastern from the western part of North America. Native Americans of the Blackfeet tribe once controlled the steep mountain passes of the Continental Divide, preventing other tribes from reaching the buffalo that grazed the plains on the eastern side. Today the Blackfeet who live on a nearby reservation play an important role in preservation efforts and managing the park's complex ecosystem.

Glacier National Park is abundant with stunning plant and animal life. Alpine flowers and a variety of pine trees grow at different altitudes throughout the park. Mountain goats come by the hundreds to lick the salt that oozes out from a huge sloping stone in one area of the park.

In 1932, Glacier National Park was joined with its northern neighbor, the Waterton Lakes national Park of Alberta, Canada, to form the Waterton-Glacier International Peace Park. The splendid vistas of these two parks remind us of what we have to lose if we do not continue to preserve our natural treasures.

The Lewis Overthrust at Glacier National Park rose up millions
of years ago from a crack in the earth.

MONTEZUMA'S CASTLE
AND HOVENWEEP

The well-preserved buildings hidden in the side of the 150-foot-high cliff in central Arizona were rumored to have been built for the Aztec Emperor Montezuma. The site probably had nothing to do with the legendary ruler, but the name has remained, and Montezuma's Castle was established as a National Monument in 1906.

Protected by the cave in which it is located, Montezuma's Castle was in excellent condition when it was first discovered. While many ancient cliff dwellings had been vandalized by pot hunters, the structures of Montezuma's Castle have been preserved just as they appeared when first built.

Montezuma's Well is a large spring-fed sink-hole near the cliff dwellings. This unusual source of water was used for the irrigation of crops raised by the Native Americans who lived here.

Another national monument established to protect an important archaeological site is Hovenweep, on the Colorado-Utah border. This is an ancient Native American village where many stone towers stand on the rim of a canyon.

Since the site has not been fully excavated, our knowledge of it is limited. The huge stone towers of Hovenweep may have been places of refuge for the villagers when they were under attack. Or perhaps the towers were built to guard valuable water sources.

Many of the Hovenweep towers have unusual shapes. Recent observations have found that they functioned both as observatories for the heavens and as markers for sunrise and sunset patterns during different times of the year.

Archaeologists are only beginning to discover evidence of how ancient Native American structures were designed to provide information about astronomical events. The protection given to these sites as national monuments will permit archaeologists to continue probing their secrets in the future.

Montezuma's Castle is hidden away in the side of a 150-foot-high cliff in central Arizona.

YOSEMITE NATIONAL PARK

Row upon row of giant Sequoia (se-COY-ya) trees dominate the landscape at Yosemite, in California. Many individuals and organizations who recognized the special beauty of Yosemite fought to have this area protected and preserved. It was established as a national park in 1890.

Some of the Sequoias are as many as 3,000 years old. Many of them are ten feet in diameter and more than one hundred feet tall. One of the largest trees has a tunnel cut through its base. People arriving at Yosemite by stagecoach used to drive through this opening on their way into the park. Over the years, the Sequoias have survived earthquakes, forest fires, deliberate destruction by tourists, and efforts by logging companies to cut them down. Today, three groves of these magnificent trees stand protected in Yosemite National Park.

Rivers and glaciers once carved out magnificent valleys in the area. Standing at Glacier Point, 3,200 feet above the valley floor, visitors have a spectacular view of the park below. There, stone formations polished by glaciers shimmer brilliantly in the sun. Large masses of rock split by subterranean pressures stand in interesting shapes: "Half Dome Rock" was created when forces within the dome-shaped rock caused it to split in half; "El Capitán" is a huge granite formation that rises to a height of 3,593 feet. The sheer cliff walls of El Capitán are a favorite challenge of ambitious rock climbers. Elsewhere in the park, visitors may see breath-taking waterfalls. The falls of the Upper Yosemite River drop 1,430 feet from the top of an enormous cliff.

The mountains and the valley seen from Glacier Point have inspired many artists and photographers to represent Yosemite's grandeur in their works.

Ancient Sequoia trees stand more than one hundred feet tall at Yosemite National Park.

THE GRAND TETONS

The jagged, snow-capped peaks of Wyoming's Teton Mountains rise to a height of more than 13,000 feet. No foothills buttress the eastern slope of the Tetons. The absence of foothills lends a dramatic appearance to the mountains as they rise straight up from the valley floor.

This unique geological formation is the product of what is known as a "block fault." Millions of years ago, forces within the earth split the land mass into two sections. One of these sections was pushed up while the other sank to a much lower level. The enormous block of stone that rose up from the valley floor was then subjected to the forces of erosion. Rain, wind, and glacial activity shaped the elevated block into the jagged peaks we see today. When the glaciers melted, they left behind a series of beautiful lakes. The section of the block that sank became the valley floor of the area that is now known as "Jackson Hole."

To the early trappers, a hole meant a valley. David E. Jackson, a fur trapper, is believed to have spent the winter of 1829 in the valley that now bears his name. The Snake River flows along the valley floor, and sites on the river offer spectacular views of the Teton peaks. Glaciers may be seen hanging from the mountain tops.

Like many other areas of the West, the Grand Tetons and Jackson Hole became a paradise for hunters and fishermen. People bought land for private use in this scenic area. Eventually, steps had to be taken to preserve and protect this region from private exploitation. As President of the United States, Grover Cleveland began to set aside some of the lands in the Teton region. Later, in 1929, Congress added more land to the reserve and created the Grand Teton National Park.

Impressed by the beauty of the Tetons, oil man John D. Rockefeller bought land in Jackson Hole and donated it to the federal government. His contribution provided the new land areas that make up the park today. Rockefeller added 33,000 acres of land to the park.

At the base of the Grand Tetons are many beautiful lakes that were left behind
when glaciers melted from the mountains.

MESA VERDE AND CHACO CANYON

Two spectacular areas that feature the ruins of ancient Native American civilizations are Mesa Verde National Park in southern Colorado and Chaco Canyon National Monument in northern New Mexico.

Mesa Verde features stone ruins that were once the home of the ancient Anasazi culture. The Anasazi, or "ancient ones," occupied cave sites in the canyon walls of the long mesa ridges. They built towers, houses, and storage areas in the caves that are found throughout the region.

Visitors to Mesa Verde may climb a thirty-foot-high ladder to reach an isolated dwelling called Balcony House, named after a projecting balcony that connects several buildings in the complex. Access to areas of Balcony House are through tiny openings in the rock where only one person could pass at a time. This served to protect occupants from raids by large groups of invaders.

Cliff Palace is another remarkable site at Mesa Verde. An enormous cave opening holds one of the largest displays of towers, cliff houses, and kivas in the West. Visitors may walk along the buildings, climb ladders to different levels of the cave, and peer inside the towers where prehistoric paintings are still visible on the walls

Chaco Canyon is the location of twelve ancient Anasazi communities. At each site, buildings of stone reveal places where people lived and worked. The largest of these stone communities is called "Pueblo Bonito," which is Spanish for "beautiful town." Some of the buildings in Pueblo Bonito are three or four stories high. Nearly eight hundred rooms may be seen at this magnificent site. The largest building takes the shape of the letter "D," and it is positioned so that it receives the most sun, for warmth, in the winter. Other buildings at the site are situated to measure the movements of the sun, moon, and other planets.

The multi-storied buildings of Pueblo Bonito surround a central plaza where a number of kivas may be seen. Some archaeologists believe that the site may have been a major religious shrine that attracted pilgrims from far and wide. To the modern visitor, the gigantic stone structures of Pueblo Bonito are a tribute to the architectural genius of the Anasazi people.

Pueblo Bonito, at Chaco Canyon, is a well preserved example of an ancient Anasazi community.

FOR FURTHER READING

The Alamo. Leonard Everett Fisher. New York: Holiday House, 1987.

The American Heritage Book of Indians. William Brandon. New York: Crown, 1988.

America's Fascinating Indian Heritage. Reader's Digest Association Editors. Pleasantville, New York: Reader's Digest, 1990.

Annie Oakley and Buffalo Bill's Wild West: One Hundred Two Illustrations. Isabelle S. Sayers. New York: Dover, 1981.

Canyon Country Parklands: Treasures of the Great Plateau. Scott Thybony. Washington, D.C.: National Geographic Society, 1993.

Exploring the West. Herman J. Viola. New York: Abrams, 1988.

History of Western American Art. Royal B. Hassrick. New York: Simon & Schuster, 1987.

Into the Wilderness. Donald J. Crump, Ed. Washington, D.C.: National Geographic Society, 1978.

The Oregon Trail. Leonard Everett Fisher. New York: Holiday House, 1990.

Pueblos: Prehistoric Indian Cultures of the Southwest. Sylvio Acatos and Maximilien Bruggman. New York: Facts on File, 1990.

Story of the Great American West. Reader's Digest Editors. Pleasantville, New York: Reader's Digest, 1981.

To the Inland Empire. Stewart L. Udall. New York: Doubleday, 1987.

The West. Thomas G. Aylesworth and Virginia L. Aylesworth. New York: Chelsea House, 1988.

The World of the American Indian. Jules B. Billard, Ed. Washington, D.C.: National Geographic Society, 1989.

Yosemite: An American Treasure. Donald J. Crump, Ed. Washington, D.C.: National Geographic Society, 1990.

UNIVERSITY OF RHODE ISLAND

3 1222 01041 826 0

NO LONGER THE PROPERTY OF THE UNIVERSITY OF R.I. LIBRARY

The Running Press Start Exploring™ Series
Color Your World

With crayons, markers and imagination, you can re-create works of art and discover the worlds of science, nature, and literature. Each book is $8.95 and is available from your local bookstore. If your bookstore does not have the volume you want, ask your bookseller to order it for you (or send a check/money order for the cost of each book plus $2.50 postage and handling to Running Press).

THE AGE OF DINOSAURS

by Donald F. Glut

Discover new theories about dinosaurs and learn how paleontologists work in this fascinating expedition to a time when reptiles ruled the land.

ARCHITECTURE

by Peter Dobrin

Tour 60 world-famous buildings around the world and learn their stories.

BULFINCH'S MYTHOLOGY

Retold by Steven Zorn

An excellent introduction to classical literature, with 16 tales of adventure.

FOLKTALES OF NATIVE AMERICANS

Retold by David Borgenicht

Traditional myths, tales, and legends, from more than 12 Native American peoples.

FORESTS

by Elizabeth Corning Dudley, Ph.D.

Winner, *Parents' Choice*
"Learning and Doing Award"

The first ecological coloring book, written by a respected botanist.

GRAY'S ANATOMY

by Fred Stark, Ph.D.

Winner, *Parents' Choice*
"Learning and Doing Award"

A voyage of discovery through the human body, based on the classic work.

INSECTS

by George S. Glenn, Jr.

Discover the secrets of familiar and more unusual insects.

MASTERPIECES

by Mary Martin and Steven Zorn

Line drawings and lively descriptions of 60 world-famous paintings and their artists.

MASTERPIECES OF AMERICAN ART

From the National Museum of American Art, Smithsonian Institution
by Alan Gartenhaus

Sixty ready-to-color masterpieces and their stories, including contemporary works.

OCEANS

by Diane M. Tyler and James C. Tyler, Ph.D.

Winner, *Parents' Choice*
"Learning and Doing Award"

An exploration of the life-giving seas, in expert text and 60 pictures.

PLACES OF MYSTERY

by Emmanuel M. Kramer

An adventurous tour of the most mysterious places on Earth, with more than 50 stops along the way.

SPACE

by Dennis Mammana

Share the discoveries of history's greatest space scientists and explorers.